MW00680334

Sugar Sisters

Sugar Sisters

Desserts for the Naughty and Nice

A Chicklits Book

shared by
Sugar Sister Kate Hart

CONARI PRESS

First published in 2005 by Conari Press,
an imprint of Red Wheel/Weiser, LLC
York Beach, ME
With offices at:
368 Congress Street
Boston, MA 02210
www.redwheelweiser.com

Acknowledgements on page 62.
ISBN: 1-57324-260-8

Typeset in TheSans, SignPainter, Ogre, Pike, and Cafe Mimi
by Jill Feron, FeronDesign

Printed in China
C&C Offset Printing Co., Ltd.

11 10 09 08 07 06 05
8 7 6 5 4 3 2 1

"Invention, my dear friends,
is 93% perspiration,
6% electricity,
4% evaporation, and
2% butterscotch ripple."

—WILLY WONKA

Let Them Eat Cake!

Lemon Geranium Sponge Cake 8
Chocolate Insanity Cake 10
Pineapple Upside-Down Cake 12
Angel Food Cake 14
Red Velvet Cake 16
Dundee Cake 18

Fruity Favorites

Rosy Apple Pie 20
Surefire Rhubarb Strawberry Crisp 22
Easy Chocolate-Dipped Fruit 24
Missen's Lemon Bars 26
Best-Ever Banana Cream Pie 28
Key Lime Pie 30
Stuffed Baked Peaches 32

Calling All Chocoholics

One Smart Cookie

COOKIES

Let Them Eat Cake!

Lemon Geranium Sponge Cake

This old-fashioned treat can be made any time of the year.

1/3 cup honey
3 tablespoons flour
1/4 cup fresh lemon juice
1 teaspoon grated lemon rind
2 eggs, separated
1 cup milk
5 drops geranium oil
rose geranium leaves, optional

Preheat oven to 325°F. Beat together honey, flour, lemon juice, and rind. Add yolks, milk, and geranium oil and mix again. In a separate bowl, beat egg whites until stiff, and fold into the lemon mixture. Pour into a buttered 8-inch baking pan and place in another pan of hot water. If available, lay fresh rose geranium leaves on top. Bake for 45-50 minutes, or until cake is set and knife comes out clean. Serve warm. Serves 6.

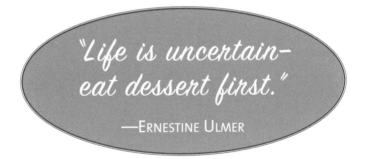

"Life is uncertain— eat dessert first."

—ERNESTINE ULMER

"My therapist told me the way to achieve
true inner peace is to finish what I start.
So far today, I have finished two bags of M&M's
and a chocolate cake. I feel better already."

—DAVE BARRY

Chocolate Insanity Cake

1 18.25-ounce package dark chocolate cake mix
1 3.9-ounce package instant chocolate pudding mix
1 16-ounce container sour cream
3 eggs
1/3 cup vegetable oil
1/2 cup coffee-flavored liqueur
2 cups semisweet chocolate chips

Preheat oven to 350°F. Grease and flour a 10-inch Bundt pan. In a large bowl, combine cake mix, pudding mix, sour cream, eggs, oil, and coffee liqueur. Beat until ingredients are well blended. Fold in chocolate chips. Batter will be thick. Spoon into prepared pan. Bake in preheated oven for 1 hour, or until cake springs back when lightly tapped. Cool 10 minutes in pan, then turn out and cool completely on wire rack.

Pineapple Upside-Down Cake

A packaged mix, the size for a single-layer or loaf cake, may be used instead of the homemade batter. The pineapple and brown sugar will get all the attention anyway.

1/4 cup (1/2 stick) butter
3/4 cup packed brown sugar
7 canned pineapple rings, drained
7 maraschino cherries
1/2 cup pecans or walnuts
1/3 cup shortening
2/3 cup granulated sugar
1 teaspoon vanilla
2 eggs
1 2/3 cups all-purpose flour
2 teaspoons baking powder
1/4 teaspoon salt
2/3 cup milk

Preheat oven to 350°F. Melt butter in a 9- or 10-inch cast iron or other ovenproof skillet. Sprinkle in the brown sugar and cook over medium heat, stirring, until melted and bubbling. Remove from heat. Arrange pineapple slices in the bottom of the pan, with a cherry in the center of each slice. Fit nuts in between slices.

In a large bowl, cream shortening with granulated sugar. Add vanilla and eggs and beat until fluffy. Stir together flour, baking powder, and salt. Add flour mixture to the creamed mixture alternately with the milk, beating until batter is smooth.

Carefully spoon the batter over the pineapple slices. Bake in oven for 35 to 45 minutes, until a skewer inserted in the center comes out clean. Remove from oven and let stand for 5 minutes. Place a serving plate face down over skillet. Using pot holders or oven mitts to protect hands, turn both upside down and remove the skillet.

Angel Food Cake

Fabulous with the boiled frosting recipe from the ultra-classic *Joy of Cooking*. And low-fat! Well, maybe not the frosting . . .

1 1/4 cups cake flour
1/2 cup sugar
12 egg whites at room temperature
1/4 teaspoon salt
1 1/4 teaspoons cream of tartar
1 teaspoon vanilla
1/4 teaspoon almond extract
1 1/3 cups sugar

Preheat oven to 375°F. Sift flour with 1/2 cup sugar four times. In a separate, large bowl, combine egg whites, salt, cream of tartar, vanilla, and almond extract. Beat with a flat wire whip, rotary beater, or high speed of electric mixer until moist, glossy, soft peaks form. Add 1 1/3 cups sugar, sprinkling in 1/3 cup at a time and beating until blended after each addition, about 25 strokes by hand. Sift in flour mixture in four additions, folding in by hand after each addition and turning bowl often. After last addition, use 10 to 20 extra strokes. Pour into ungreased 10-inch tube pan. Bake for 35 to 40 minutes, or until the top springs back when pressed lightly. Invert on rack and cool thoroughly, then remove from pan. Serve with frosting of your choice. Serves 8.

Red Velvet Cake

1/2 cup butter, margarine, or shortening
1 1/2 cups sugar
2 eggs
1 teaspoon vanilla
3 tablespoons cocoa
2 ounces red food coloring
2 1/2 cups sifted cake flour
1 cup buttermilk
1 teaspoon salt
1 teaspoon baking soda
1 tablespoon white vinegar

Preheat oven to 350°F. Cream shortening and sugar until smooth. Add eggs and vanilla. Beat well. In a separate bowl, blend cocoa and food coloring; add to sugar mixture. Add flour, buttermilk, and salt alternatively. Mix soda and vinegar in cup and add to batter. Bake in two greased and floured 9-inch cake pans for 30 to 35 minutes or until a toothpick inserted in the center comes out clean. Let cool before frosting.

"Your good friend has just taken a piece of cake out of the garbage and eaten it. You will probably need this information when you check me into the Betty Crocker Clinic."

—MIRANDA, LEAVING A VOICEMAIL MESSAGE ON *SEX AND THE CITY*

Dundee Cake

1 cup flour
1 teaspoon baking powder
3/4 cup butter
1/2 cup granulated sugar
4 eggs
1 ounce blanched almonds
1 1/2 ounces mixed orange and lemon peel
3/4 cup each currants, raisins, and seedless white raisins
grated rind and juice of 1 lemon
2 tablespoons water
1 tablespoon boiled milk with 1 tablespoon sugar stirred in

Preheat oven to 325°F. In a small bowl, sift the flour and baking powder together. Set aside. In a large bowl, cream the butter and sugar until fluffy, then add the eggs one at a time. Stir in the nuts, fruits, and lemon rind and juice. Add the flour mixture and the water, and mix well. Place mixture in an 8-inch greased and lined cake tin. Flatten the top with damp hands. Cover with foil and bake for 2 hours or until a tester poked in the middle comes out clean. Ten minutes before cake is done, brush the top with the sweetened milk. Cool in the pan for 15 minutes before turning out on a wire tray. Serves 8.

Fruity Favorites

Rosy Apple Pie

3/4 cup sugar
1/2 cup water
1/4 cup red cinnamon candies, like Red-Hots!
5 medium cooking apples (about 5 cups apple slices)
1 tablespoon flour
1 teaspoon lemon juice
1 tablespoon butter or margarine
9-inch double pie crust (frozen is fine)

Preheat oven to 400°F. In a medium saucepan, combine sugar, water, and cinnamon candies; cook until candies dissolve. Pare, core, and slice apples. Add to sugar mixture and simmer until apples are red. Drain but save syrup. Blend flour into cooled syrup and add lemon juice. Spread apples in a pastry-lined 9-inch pie plate and pour syrup over apples. Dot with butter. Cover with top crust, seal, and flute edges. Cut slits for steam to escape. Bake about 30 minutes until desired brownness. Makes 1 pie.

The old wives' tale is true.

According to a study done by Michigan State University, those who eat apples daily get fewer respiratory infections than those who don't.

Surefire Rhubarb Strawberry Crisp

3 cups rhubarb, sliced
2 cups strawberries, whole or sliced
juice from one lemon
1 stick butter, softened
1 cup granulated sugar
1 cup flour

Preheat oven to 400°F. Combine rhubarb, strawberries, and lemon juice in a 9 x 13-inch baking pan. In a medium bowl, combine the butter, sugar, and flour until crumbly and then spread over rhubarb mixture. Bake uncovered for 20 minutes or until crisp is bubbly and top browned. Serves 6.

Need to get your strawberry groove on?

Try visiting Wepion, Belgium, the world capital of strawberries and stop by the World Famous Strawberry Museum. Or, maybe a little closer to home, visit Plant City, Florida—the winter strawberry capital of the world.

Easy Chocolate-Dipped Fruit

1 ounce (2 squares) bittersweet chocolate, chopped
1/2 tablespoon whipping cream
dash of almond extract
8 fresh strawberries, figs, banana slices, cookies, or any-
   thing else you'd like to dip in chocolate

Combine chocolate and cream in a glass measuring cup or
bowl; microwave for 1 minute at medium heat, stirring
after 30 seconds, or until the chocolate melts. Stir in the
almond extract and cool slightly. Dip each piece of fruit or
cookie into the melted chocolate, allowing any excess to
drip off. Place on waxed paper and refrigerate for approximately 15 minutes or until the chocolate is set.

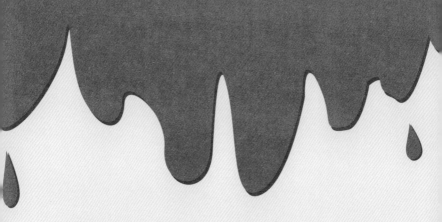

"Chocolate-covered raisins, cherries, orange slices, and strawberries all count as fruit, so make sure you get enough."

—THERESA CHEUNG,
IN HER CHOCOGRAPHY *BETTER THAN SEX*

Missen's Lemon Bars

Named for a friend's daughter, who—after grabbing her share of the lemon bars—is usually "Missen—as in gone."

Crust
2 cups unbleached white flour
1/2 cup sugar
1 cup butter, at room temperature

Lemon Filling
1 1/2 cups sugar
1/4 cup unbleached white flour
juice and finely grated rind of 3 lemons
1 teaspoon baking powder
3 eggs
powdered sugar for decoration

Preheat oven to 350°F. Mix crust ingredients together and press into a greased, 9 x 13-inch glass baking dish. Bake for 10 to 15 minutes. Cool for 10 minutes before adding filling. For filling, mix all ingredients together and pour over the cooled crust. Bake for 20 to 30 minutes. Sprinkle powdered sugar on top after lemon bars have cooled (at least 15 minutes) and cut while in the pan. Makes 18 bars.

Best-Ever Banana Cream Pie

1 9-inch pie crust
3 cups whole milk
2/3 cup sugar
4 egg yolks
1/4 cup cornstarch
1 package (8 ounces) cream cheese
1 teaspoon vanilla extract
2 teaspoons dark rum or rum extract
pinch of nutmeg
3 medium bananas, ripe yet firm
juice of half a lemon
1 cup whipping cream
1 teaspoon sugar

On average, Americans eat 25 pounds of bananas annually. Maybe that's because they are good at alleviating depression—they contain the mood elevators serotonin and norepinephrine.

Bake the pie crust at 400°F for 7 to 9 minutes, cool and set aside.

Combine the milk, sugar, egg yolks, and cornstarch in a heavy saucepan and whisk madly until mixture is frothy. Cook, stirring constantly, over low heat until mixture begins to boil and thickens enough to coat a metal spoon lightly. Add cream cheese and stir until melted, about 2 minutes. Remove from heat and add vanilla, rum or rum extract, and nutmeg. Let cool to room temperature.

Slice the bananas and arrange them on the bottom of the baked pie shell. Sprinkle a wee bit of lemon juice over the bananas if you feel the urge. Pour the cooled custard over the bananas and chill for at least 2 hours.

Just before serving, whip the cream and sugar together until stiff, and garnish the pie with whipped cream. Serves 8.

Key Lime Pie

1 prepared graham cracker, chocolate Oreo cookie, or
   vanilla wafer pie crust
1 8-ounce package cream cheese, room temperature
1 12-ounce can sweetened condensed milk
1/2 cup real key lime juice
1 cup whipping cream or prepared whipped cream topping

You can either prepare a pie crust according to a favorite recipe or purchase one that is already made. My favorite crust for this pie is the chocolate Oreo cookie crust. If using "real" whipped cream, whip cream until stiff. In another large bowl, combine cream cheese and milk and whip together until smooth. Beat in key lime juice. Gently fold in whipped cream. Pour ingredients into pie shell and chill for at least one hour (you can put it in the freezer for a quick chill if desired).

Always taste your first bite of this pie with your eyes closed.

It's sensational!

Stuffed Baked Peaches

10 fresh peaches, pitted and halved
1 egg yolk
7 tablespoons butter, softened
1 cup crushed Amaretto di Saronni cookies

Remove one spoonful of peach flesh from each peach and puree; set aside. Cream 6 tablespoons of butter in a bowl, stirring in egg yolk, peach puree, and crushed cookies until well combined. Fill each peach half with a generously rounded scoop of the mixture.

Preheat oven to 375°F. Place the peach halves, open side up, in a large glass casserole with the remaining tablespoon of butter, and bake for 5-7 minutes or until cookie mixture is lightly browned. Serve peaches at room temperature with creme fraiche or ice cream. Serves 10.

"In Hollywood,
the women are all peaches.
It makes one long for
an apple occasionally."

—W. Somerset Maugham

Calling All Chocoholics

In the villages of Central America during the eighteenth century, chocolate was believed to be the drink of the devil, and no one under 60 was allowed to imbibe under threat of excommunication.

Truffles

12 ounces bittersweet chocolate, chopped
1/3 cup heavy cream
1 teaspoon vanilla extract, almond extract,
   or any other flavoring
powdered sugar, cocoa powder, sprinkles, or
   chopped nuts for decoration

Combine chocolate and cream in a medium saucepan over medium heat. Cook, stirring until chocolate is melted and mixture is smooth. Remove from heat and whisk in flavoring. Pour into a small dish and refrigerate until set, but not hard, 1 1/2 to 2 hours. Form balls and roll in toppings. Makes 35 truffles.

> "Research tells us that
> 14 out of any 10 individuals
> like chocolate."
>
> —Sandra Boynton

Mousse au Chocolat

8 ounces bittersweet chocolate, broken into pieces
2 teaspoons vanilla
8 tablespoons unsalted butter, cut up into pieces
1/2 cup sugar, preferably superfine
8 egg yolks
5 egg whites

Put the chocolate and vanilla in a double boiler over gently boiling water. Stir until melted, then remove from heat. Add the butter and stir until melted. In a large bowl, beat the sugar and egg yolks until thick. Add the chocolate. In a separate bowl, beat the egg whites until stiff. Add about a third of the egg whites to the chocolate mixture and beat until well mixed. Gradually fold in the remaining egg whites, and this time, mix gently rather than vigorously. Blend well, but do not overmix. Pour the mixture into a large serving bowl and cover with plastic wrap. Refrigerate at least 7 hours before serving. Serves 8.

"I don't love acting.
I love chocolate."

—Elizabeth Taylor

Bad-Girl Brownies

Preheat oven to 325°F. Melt 4 squares of bittersweet chocolate in a pan with 1 stick of butter. Set aside and let it cool. When it's room temp add:

2 scant cups of sugar
2 cups of flour
4 eggs
1 teaspoon of vanilla, almond, or cherry extract

Don't stir too much! Only until mixed.

Bake for 30 minutes in a lightly greased 9 x 12-inch cake pan.

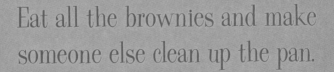

Eat all the brownies and make
someone else clean up the pan.

Easy Chocolate Soufflé

1/4 cup unsalted butter
5 squares semisweet chocolate, chopped
3 eggs, separated
1/2 cup sugar
1/2 cup flour
2 tablespoons cocoa powder
1/2 teaspoon vanilla
whipped cream or raspberry sauce for garnish

Preheat oven to 375°F. Heat butter and chocolate together until completely melted (you can do this in the microwave for about 2 minutes). Stir until smoothly blended. In a separate bowl, beat egg whites at medium speed until foamy, then gradually beat in sugar. Continue beating until stiff peaks form. Add yolks, flour, cocoa powder, and vanilla to the chocolate mixture. Gently fold in approximately a third of the egg white mixture, then gradually add the remainder. Spoon into four 6-ounce ramekins or a baking dish, and bake 15 to 20 minutes on a jelly roll pan until tops are puffed. Top with whipped cream or raspberry sauce. Serves 4.

"All I really need is love, but a little chocolate now and then doesn't hurt!"

—LUCY VAN PELT IN CHARLES M. SCHULZ'S *PEANUTS*

No Brown M&M's for These Rock Stars!

M&M's were supposedly developed so that soldiers in the field could eat candy without getting covered in chocolate. First sold in 1941, they quickly became a favorite of GIs serving in World War II.

The colors of the M&M rainbow have caused many a controversy; some say the GREEN ONES are an APHRODISIAC, others say the ORANGE ONES INCREASE BREAST SIZE. Even some celebrities have gotten in on the M&M color craze. The band VAN HALEN so hated brown M&M's that it was written into their contract that if they even saw one as they were about to play a concert, they would leave.

Mexican Hot Chocolate

2 ounces unsweetened chocolate
2 cups milk
1 cup heavy cream
6 tablespoons sugar
1/2 to 1 teaspoon ground cinnamon
1 teaspoon pure vanilla extract

In a double boiler, melt the chocolate. In a separate pot over medium-low heat, heat the milk and cream until hot but not boiled. Be careful not to scorch. When the milk is hot, add a bit to the melted chocolate and mix well. Then stir in the rest of the milk, and add the sugar, cinnamon, and vanilla. With the double boiler over low heat, beat the chocolate mixture with an electric mixer on low or a rotary mixer for three minutes. Taste and add more cinnamon if desired. Serve immediately. Serves 4.

"In the 18th century, the legendary Casanova drank chocolate instead of champagne and declared it the elixir of love."

—THERESA CHEUNG, IN HER CHOCOGRAPHY *BETTER THAN SEX*

Chocolate Cupcakes

1/3 cup all-purpose flour
6 ounces sugar
2 eggs plus 1 yolk
3 1/2 ounces butter
3 ounces semisweet chocolate
A pinch of salt

Combine the flour and sugar in a large bowl. Add the eggs and the extra yolk, and beat until smooth.

In a small heavy saucepan over medium-low heat, melt the butter and chocolate together with the salt. Remove from heat and combine with the flour mixture. Refrigerate for 3 hours.

Preheat the oven to 375°F. Scoop the batter into greased cupcake tins and bake until a toothpick inserted in the center comes out clean, about 20 minutes. Makes 1 dozen cupcakes.

One Smart Cookie

"Seize the moment. Remember all those women on the Titanic who waved off the dessert cart."

—ERMA BOMBECK

Killer Sugar Cookies

1 cup butter
2 cups sugar
3 eggs
1 cup buttermilk
1/4 cup vanilla extract
1 teaspoon baking soda
4 1/2 cups flour sifted
1 tablespoon plus 1 teaspoon baking powder

Preheat oven to 350°F. Cream sugar and butter. Add the wet ingredients. Sift in dry ingredients while beating slowly until just blended. Let dough sit at room temperature for ten minutes to rest. Drop onto greased cookie sheets and sprinkle with colored sugar. Bake 10 minutes. Cookies will seem undone, just let them sit and they will be fine.

Margie's Ultimate Chocolate Chip Classics

1/2 cup margarine at room temperature
1/2 cup butter at room temperature
1 cup brown sugar
1 cup white sugar
2 eggs
1 teaspoon pure vanilla extract
1/2 teaspoon salt
1 teaspoon baking soda
1 teaspoon baking powder
3 cups unbleached white flour
2 cups chocolate chips

Preheat oven to 350°F. In a large mixing bowl, and using an electric mixer, whip up margarine, butter, and sugars until fluffy. Add the eggs, vanilla, and salt, and mix well.

Blend the baking soda, baking powder, and flour, either directly in the measuring cup or in a large bowl, and tap into the creamed mixture, beating on low speed. With a strong wooden spoon, stir in the chocolate chips.

Line a cookie sheet with baking parchment and scoop the dough with a small ice cream scoop. Press the top of the cookie dough mound oh-so-slightly. Cast your spell over the first tray of chippers and bake for 9 to 11 minutes, until lightly golden in color with tiny cracks on top of the cookies. Makes 2 dozen.

TIP:
If you're aiming for an even more delicate, melt-in-your-mouth-but-crunchy crust and an ecstatically gooey inside, substitute 1 1/4 cups oat flour for 1 cup of the unbleached white flour.

Mexican Wedding Cookies

1/2 cup powdered sugar
1 cup butter at room temperature
1 teaspoon vanilla
2 1/4 cups flour
1/4 teaspoon salt
3/4 cup chopped nuts, optional
additional powdered sugar for decoration

Cream together the half cup of powdered sugar, butter, and vanilla in a large bowl. Sift in the flour and salt. Add the nuts, if using. Cover and chill the dough for 2 hours in the refrigerator or 10 minutes in the freezer.

Preheat oven to 400°F. Roll the dough into 1-inch balls and place on an ungreased cookie sheet. Bake until set, about 10 minutes. While still warm, roll the cookies in powdered sugar. Makes 4 dozen.

Peanut Butter Crisscross

1 cup margarine, at room temperature
1 cup white sugar
1 cup packed brown sugar
3 eggs
1 teaspoon pure vanilla extract
1/4 teaspoon salt
1 3/4 cups peanut butter, chunky or smooth
1 teaspoon baking soda
3 cups unbleached white flour

Preheat oven to 350°F. In a large mixing bowl, beat the margarine and sugars until fluffy. Add the eggs, vanilla, and salt and mix well. Gently mix in the peanut butter. Blend the baking soda into the flour, either directly in the measuring cup or in a bowl, and tap flour into the creamed mixture, stirring slowly until well blended.

With a small ice cream scoop, scoop out 1- to 2-ounce balls of dough onto a parchment-lined cookie sheet. With a 4-tined fork, press the top of the cookie gently to make a classic crisscross design. Bake for 8 to 10 minutes until golden. Take a bite and zoom back to your childhood. Makes approximately 2 dozen cookies.

"I am still convinced that a good, simple, homemade cookie is preferable to all the store-bought cookies one can find."

—JAMES BEARD

Bring on the Ginger! Cookies

Spicy and bold and with three kinds of ginger, there is no way to ignore the dynamic taste of these treats.

3/4 cup unsalted butter, at room temperature
1 cup packed dark brown sugar
1/4 cup molasses
1 egg
2 cups unbleached flour
2 teaspoons ground ginger
2 teaspoons baking soda
1/2 teaspoon salt
1 1/2 tablespoons chopped ginger root
1/2 cup finely chopped crystallized ginger

Cream together butter and brown sugar in a large mixing bowl. Beat in molasses and then egg. Sift flour, ground ginger, baking soda, and salt. Stir into butter mixture with a wooden spoon until blended. Add other gingers and mix well. Refrigerate dough for at least 2 hours or overnight.

Preheat oven to 350°F and grease cookie sheets. Shape the dough into 1-inch balls and place on cookie sheet about 2 inches apart. Bake until browned, about 10 minutes. Remove to racks and cool completely. Makes about 4 dozen.

"Think what a better world
it would be if we all, the whole
world, had cookies and milk about
three o'clock every afternoon
and then lay down on our
blankets for a nap."
—BARBARA JORDAN

Chinese Almond Cookies

1/2 cup whole roasted almonds
1 cup sifted all-purpose flour
1/2 teaspoon baking powder
1/4 teaspoon salt
1/2 cup butter or margarine
1/3 cup granulated sugar
1/2 teaspoon almond extract
1 tablespoon water

Preheat oven to 350°F and grease several cookie sheets. Reserve 36 whole almonds; finely chop or grind remainder. Sift flour with baking powder and salt. Thoroughly cream butter and sugar in a large bowl. Stir in all remaining ingredients except whole almonds. Form dough into 36 balls. Place on greased cookie sheets. Press a whole almond in the center of each ball, or dot with a bit of red food coloring. Bake for 20 minutes or until lightly browned. Makes about 3 dozen.

Chow Mein Haystacks

My mom makes these for the holidays. She almost always has to make a second batch—after I devour the first one. Try with an icy cold glass of milk.

1 12-ounce bag semisweet chocolate chips
1 12-ounce bag butterscotch chips
5 ounces chow mein noodles
6 ounces cocktail peanuts

Melt the chocolate chips and butterscotch chips over a double boiler. Remove from heat and add the noodles and peanuts; mix in well, but don't overmix as the noodles will start to break. Drop by teaspoonful onto a cookie sheet covered in wax paper. Chill in the freezer until hardened, about 15 minutes.

"A balanced diet is a cookie in each hand."

—Anonymous

Sugar Sisters Acknowledgments

Grateful acknowledgment is made to the following for permission to reprint material copyrighted by them. All reprinted by permission of Red Wheel/Weiser.

Alicia Alvrez, *The Ladies' Room Reader Revisited*. Boston, MA: Conari Press, an imprint of Red Wheel/Weiser, 2002. On page 43.

The Editors of Conari Press, *Weekends Away*. Boston, MA: Conari Press, an imprint of Red Wheel/Weiser, 2002. On pages 18-19, 36-37.

Hailey Klein, *For Goddess' Sake*. Boston, MA: Conari Press, an imprint of Red Wheel/Weiser, 2004. On pages 24, 56-57.

Margie Lapanja, *The Goddess' Guide to Love*. Boston, MA: Conari Press, an imprint of Red Wheel/Weiser, 1999. On pages 30-31.

Margie Lapanga, *Romancing the Stove*. Boston, MA: Conari Press, an imprint of Red Wheel/Weiser, 2003.
On pages 26-29, 50-51, 54-55.

Susannah Seton, *Simple Pleasures*. Boston, MA: Conari Press, an imprint of Red Wheel/Weiser, 1996.
On pages 12-13.

Susannah Seton, *Simple Pleasures for the Holidays*. Boston, MA: Conari Press, an imprint of Red Wheel/Weiser, 2000.
On pages 14-17, 40-41, 52, 58.

Susannah Seton, *Simple Pleasures of the Garden*. Boston, MA: Conari Press, an imprint of Red Wheel/Weiser, 1998.
On pages 8-9, 22, 32.

Susannah Seton, *Simple Pleasures of the Home*. Boston, MA: Conari Press, an imprint of Red Wheel/Weiser, 1999.
On pages 20-21.

The Wild Women Association, *Wild Women in the Kitchen*. Boston, MA: Conari Press, an imprint of Red Wheel/Weiser, 1996. On pages 44, 46.